3 4028 08503 2952
HARRIS COUNTY PUBLIC LIBRARY

J 788.32 Rig
Riggs
Flute   SO-AZE-248

$7.99
ocn883419151
First edition.   09/10/2014

FLUTE

MAKING  MUSIC

KATE RIGGS

CREATIVE
PAPER BACKS

WITHDRAWN

PUBLISHED *by* Creative Paperbacks

P.O. Box 227, Mankato, Minnesota 56002

Creative Paperbacks is an imprint of The Creative Company

www.thecreativecompany.us

DESIGN AND PRODUCTION *by* Ellen Huber
ART DIRECTION *by* Rita Marshall
PRINTED *in the* United States of America

PHOTOGRAPHS *by*

Bigstock (desertsolitaire), Corbis (Chris Christodoulou/Lebrecht
Music & Arts), Dreamstime (Firststar), Getty Images (Hybrid
Images, KidStock, Christian Kober, Steve Thorne/Redferns,
Travel Ink), iStockphoto (code6d, Dennis Guillaume, Ela
Kwasniewski, Dmitry Maslov, Terry Wilson), Shutterstock
(cowardlion, Angelo Giampiccolo, Tatiana Grozetskaya,
Ela Kwasniewski, mkm3, Robynrg, Dmitry Skutin, Tadas_
Naujokaitis78, Tumar, vasi2), Veer (Mikhail Olykaynen)

Copyright © 2014 Creative Paperbacks
International copyright reserved in all countries.
No part of this book may be reproduced in any form
without written permission from the publisher.

LIBRARY OF CONGRESS
CATALOGING-IN-PUBLICATION DATA
Riggs, Kate.
Flute / Kate Riggs.
p. cm. — (Making music)
SUMMARY: *A primary prelude to the flute, including what*
the woodwind instrument looks and sounds like, basic instructions
on how to play it, and the kinds of music that feature it.
Includes bibliographical references and index.

ISBN 978-1-60818-367-8 (*hardcover*)
ISBN 978-0-89812-946-5 (*pbk*)
1. Flute—Juvenile literature. 1. Title.

ML935.R54 2013
788.3'2—DC23   2013009494

FIRST EDITION
9 8 7 6 5 4 3 2 1

TABLE OF CONTENTS

WHEN YOU HEAR A FLUTE

Cheerful birds chirping.

Gentle breezes blowing through leaves.

Sucking on a sweet piece of candy.

What do you think of when you hear a flute?

Birds such as robins have musical calls.
Wind blowing through leaves makes a whooshing sound.

THE WOODWIND FAMILY

Musical instruments that sound and

look alike belong to a "family."

Flutes are part of the woodwind family.

These instruments use air to make sounds.

A woodwind player blows air into a **reed**

or over a mouth hole.

•— *An oboe reed*

flute

piccolo

Many instruments (such as those shown) make up the woodwind family.

bassoon

saxophone

clarinet

English horn

oboe

HOW FLUTES ARE MADE

Flutes are shaped like long, hollow tubes.

Woodwind instruments were first made out of wood.

Now they are made of wood and metal.

The first all-metal flutes were made in the 1800s.

Long ago, people used thin wood such as bamboo to make flutes.

Some Chinese bamboo
flutes are called dizi
(TEET-see).

A flute's mouth hole and keys set it apart from other woodwinds.

PARTS OF A FLUTE

A flute is made up of three parts called joints.

The head joint is the part of the flute

that has the mouth hole.

The body joint has most of the **keys** on it.

The foot joint is at the end of the flute.

It is the shortest part of the flute.

head joint   body joint   foot joint

KINDS OF FLUTES

The three joints break apart to make

the flute easy to carry and store.

Flutes are about 26 inches (66 cm) long.

They are twice as big as **piccolos** (*PICK-uh-lowz*).

Piccolos sound a lot like whistles!

A piccolo breaks down into two pieces instead of three.

The parts of a flute fit inside a small case.

A piccolo is easy to carry in a marching band.

*Make the corners
of your mouth tuck in,
and blow gently.*

PLAYING THE FLUTE

A flute is held sideways in the air. You blow air

across the mouth hole. This makes a soft, breathy sound.

Your lower lip rests on the lip plate.

You use your fingers to press 13 keys that cover or

uncover holes on the side of the flute.

Your left hand holds the body joint. Your right thumb supports the foot joint.

EARLY FLUTES

People have played flutes for hundreds of years.

Flutes in some parts of the world are

still made of little pipes of different lengths.

The pipes are tied together with string or cloth.

Some tubelike flutes played in Thailand are tied together in a circle.

FLUTE MUSIC

Flutists can play the flute standing up or sitting down.

They play in orchestras (*OR-keh-struhz*)

and bands such as marching bands.

Many songs are written for **solo** flute.

A soloist stands in front of the orchestra.
Other flutists are seated (opposite).

Marching flutes have to be held just right so that they don't hit people.

THE FLUTISTS PLAY

A marching band plays at your school's football game.

All the flutists stand in a row.

The flutes chirp a high, cheerful song.

Everyone claps along, and the flutes lead the way!

MEET A FLUTIST

James Galway was born in Belfast,

Northern Ireland, in 1939. He moved to London, England,

to become a better flutist when he was a teenager.

James has played flute solos all around the world.

He likes to travel a lot and teach people about the flute.

James and his wife Jeanne

play flute together in songs called duets.

James Galway is nicknamed "The Man with the Golden Flute."

Harris County Public Library
Houston, Texas

GLOSSARY

keys: *small levers covering the holes on the side of the flute*

piccolos: *small flutes that make very high-pitched sounds*

reed: *a thin piece of wood or metal that a woodwind player blows into to make a sound*

solo: *something done for or by one person*

READ MORE

Ganeri, Anita. *Wind Instruments*.
North Mankato, Minn.: Smart Apple Media, 2012.

Levine, Robert. *The Story of the Orchestra*.
New York: Black Dog & Leventhal, 2001.

Storey, Rita. *The Recorder and Other Wind Instruments*.
North Mankato, Minn.: Smart Apple Media, 2010.

WEBSITES

Dallas Symphony Orchestra Kids
http://www.dsokids.com/default.aspx
Listen to the sounds a flute makes, play games, and make your own instrument.

YouTube: Sir James Galway Masterclass
http://www.youtube.com/
watch?v=VQgovScnQ8E&feature=relmfu
Watch James Galway show how to blow into a flute and make a good sound.

Every effort has been made to ensure that these sites are suitable for children, that they have educational value, and that they contain no inappropriate material. However, because of the nature of the Internet, it is impossible to guarantee that these sites will remain active indefinitely or that their contents will not be altered.